D1374120

BELONGINGS

The Italian Collection

Inventions of Farewell: A Book of Elegies

Kissing the Bread: New and Selected Poems, 1969–1999

Acts of Attention: The Poems of D. H. Lawrence

In the Fourth World: Poems

The Summer Kitchen: Poems

Emily's Bread: Poems

Blood Pressure: Poems

Wrongful Death: A Memoir

Ghost Volcano: Poems

The Madwoman in the Attic:
The Woman Writer and the 19th Century Literary Imagination
(with Susan Gubar)

No Man's Land:
The Place of the Woman Writer in the 20th Century
(in three volumes, with Susan Gubar)

Masterpiece Theatre: An Academic Melodrama
(with Susan Gubar)

Shakespeare's Sisters: Feminist Essays on Women Poets
(editor, with Susan Gubar)

The Norton Anthology of Literature by Women: The Tradition in English
(editor, with Susan Gubar)

The House Is Made of Poetry: Essays on the Art of Ruth Stone
(editor, with Wendy Barker)

MotherSongs: Poems For, By, and About Mothers
(editor, with Susan Gubar and Diana O'Hehir)

BELONGINGS

Poems

Sandra M. Gilbert

 W. W. Norton & Company • New York • London

811.54
G46 b

For information about permission to reproduce selections from this
book, write to Permissions, W. W. Norton & Company, Inc., 500
Fifth Avenue, New York, NY 10110

Manufacturing by Courier Westford
Book design by Mary McDonnell
Production manager: Anna Oler

Library of Congress Cataloging-in-Publication Data

Gilbert, Sandra M.
Belongings : poems / Sandra M. Gilbert.—1st ed.
p. cm.
ISBN 0-393-05990-1 (hardcover)
I. Title.
PS3557.I34227B45 2005
811'.54—dc22
2004014810
W. W. Norton & Company, Inc., 500 Fifth Avenue,
New York, N.Y. 10110
www.wwnorton.com

W. W. Norton & Company Ltd., Castle House, 75/76 Wells Street,
London W1T 3QT
1 2 3 4 5 6 7 8 9 0

For the ones to whom
I first belonged:
Alexis Joseph Mortola
and
Angela Maria Caruso

Contents

BELONGINGS

AFTERNOON WALK: THE SEA RANCH

Late light, uneven mole-gnawed meadow,
gullies, freshets, falls, whose start and speckle
Hopkins would have loved—and you—you too,
who loved the sheen and shade, the forest dapple
where grass meets cypress just beyond the house—
you'd praise the mushroom-sprout, the chilly glisten
as the hedgerow folds into the solstice
and suddenly the last crisp leaves unfasten.

This time of year, this place, light dims at the pace
of a long late afternoon walk, light seems to slow
and sorrow as the meadow turns its face
into your unlived season, the winter hollow
where only a steep sky, in quarter inches,
adjusts descending sun, ascending branches.

    —in memory of E.L.G.

I | Belongings

BELONGINGS

—in memory of Angela Maria Incoronata Caruso Mortola,
May 21, 1903–January 14, 2001

1

In-and-out sun like the light of her mind that knows
and doesn't feels and forgets pelts of rain
hide and seek of thought first gray then rose
but still a steady backlight (sometimes hidden):
"Remember Woody Allen's line? I'm not
like that I don't care when it happens where
I just don't want to die not scared not that
I just don't want to and I told the doctor!"
and the doctor laughing "Cute old lady said
she doesn't care about the why and wherefore
she just doesn't want to die . . ." and therefore?
then she forgets smiles turns her head
to nod *grande dame* at shadows on the walls
that gather where the light collects and falls

2

They gather where the light collects and falls
we can't see them but she seems to think
at least a few are smiling so she feels
she *has* to say hello politely thank
these thoughtful ghosts who visit sister brothers
Sunday best in black old Brooklyn friends
who hardly see the gulf of sixty years
mama and papa severe Sicilian bookends
"Come in, come in" her eyes light up she waves
and beckons all to chairs around her bed
so she can boast to brothers and their wives
of all the special things her daughter did
and how her grandkids won so many prizes
and as she vaunts and glows her smile blazes

3

But though she glows but though her smile blazes
the sister flickers fades the brothers falter
her eyesight's bad it's hard to see their faces
as if she peered through gauze or a thick filter
and then the *others* come the ones she calls
"co-tenants" of her rooms the lovers *screwing*
coarse as goats in corners nasty girls
smart-aleck guys who *do* know what they're doing
and what they do is occupy her place
back home they swarmed all over her apartment
set up a stove behind her lovely bookcase
nursed babies on her sofa bold indifferent
and even here still shameless in their clingings
they mean to steal they'll steal her best belongings

4

What should she do to safeguard her belongings?
she begs for help urges us to lock
to triple lock the doors to hide her things
her pearls right *here* her fruitwood in New York
her mother's hand-carved walnut chairs the leather-
surfaced desk at which my father sat
so long ago wearing the cashmere sweater
grandma bought him and the Sulka shirt
Listen! Are we listening? Have we *heard?*
How well he dressed! How beautiful their place!
four rooms in Queens what lots couldn't afford
in an age of breadlines shameful jobs or worse
"Tuono di Dio!" thunder of God she looses
the curse she learned in childhood for most uses

5

The curses learned in childhood have their uses
Tuono di Dio! she swears when they strip her bare
to bathe her *Tuono di Dio!* when the nurses
slide the soiled bed pads to the floor
or prop her in the wheelchair to be fed
thunder of God echoes along the halls
when she tries to fight the husky nurse's aide
come to sponge her bruises stains and spills
embarrassed we shiver in the corridor
while she flails and shrieks for the police
"*Tuono di Dio!* Call the police!" God's thunder
will scorch us if we leave her in this place
away from her apartment calm and peace
away from her belongings purse and keys

6

Away from her belongings purse and keys
(and crumpled Kleenex reading glasses coins
and comb she always carries in that purse)
she isn't real! she might be only bones!
yet the belongings longings must go on
the bookcase and the rugs and tables must
survive outlast her so she tells her grandson
how to plan an auction in the east
these are the costs of those belongings that
the value of mahogany and this
the price of sterling silver (which she fought
to buy—a fifth-grade teacher in the thirties—)
and the bracelets furs her in-laws gave
too bad they can't go with her to the grave!

7

What happens to belongings after the grave?
They'll be up here and she she'll be down there
what of the stuff she worked so hard to have?
polished mahogany and mink and silver
and even the fifteen-year-old television
still good still just right for the nightly news
and the brand-new vacuum cleaner even
still a— a *something* someone ought to choose
her face is crumpling like a handkerchief
don't give it all away don't give it up
if *you* don't want it at least sell it off!
don't let the *others* have it either stop
the thieves before they drag it all away
don't let my *belongings* go astray. . . .

8

Don't let *my* belongings go astray
call the super tell the doorman keep
the windows locked and barred the crooks away
the ones who break and enter when you sleep
the ones who follow sullen knife and rape
how many years she's warned us can't we hear
they'll pick the locks they'll climb the fire escape
just look the crooks are here are everywhere
a sudden nod a glance at the next bed
where a wizened person gasps and snores
that one now she saw her yes she did
peering in closets rummaging in drawers
even in hospitals they have no pity
they rob you when they see your things are pretty

9

Yet O it's nice that all her things are pretty
her smile blazes back in Jackson Heights
(on one of the better blocks in New York City)
her beautiful apartment basks and waits
a hush of rugs a drawn Venetian blind
keeping the silence keeping the bars of shadow
gathered like silent guardians around
the hanging shelf the Wedgewood the piano
and there the family photographs are massed
my father's face blade-thin in sepia
my baby self in flounces or undressed
from times when she was poor but happier
belongings blurry as if underwater
bearing the prints of mother father daughter

10

How far the age of mother father daughter!
my baby room with walls now pink now blue
(but never yellow though I begged I fought her)
and the tiny snowman globe where snowflakes flew
and the little silver Virgin Mary shrine
whose key I turned to play Our Lady's song
"Ave Maria" tinkling out of tune
and the gray hooked rug where silent bluebirds sang
and a rabbit ran away among the trees
but never vanished never could escape
whatever chased him from the knitted haze
a scary thing *because* it had no shape
though now the whole room's painted hazy gray
and the rabbit trees and birds raveled away

11

When did her mind begin to ravel away?
—that time she fell outside the beauty parlor
(getting pretty for her grandson's birthday)?
she didn't answer when we tried to call her
and soon with mop and broom she fought the *others*
called 911 the super the police
there on the sofa sat the nursing mothers
the lovers crawled and thrashed under the bookcase
we flew to Queens we packed up all her things
the fox-head furs her mother's lion-necklace
"But what about all my other best belongings?"
she worried then gave up resigned to silence
a roar of takeoff buckled in she hissed
"Here's to my new adventure in the west!"

12

At sundown tantrums shake the sunset west
the nurses turn her toward the flashing window
"See the flowers? See the pretty bird's nest?"
bushes tug in tubs on the patio
where a night wind rises over Astroturf
batters the waiting tables chairs and wheelchairs
as if they stood in a swirl of Pacific surf
whose icy water glitters darkens clears
"Here's dinner, hon!" the nurses's aide with bib
holds out a tray of lukewarm grown-up mush
last week a fall tore muscles cracked a rib
how did she fall did someone really *push?*
she tries to remember strains to see remembers
(sometimes) the names of sundown visitors

13

Sometimes the names of sundown visitors
hook into thought sometimes the sounds unravel
blur sister brothers TV commentators
(Frank and Vito turn into Ted Koppel)
I visit afternoons bring cupcakes chocolate
the only stuff she ever wants to eat
can barely swallow though one night past midnight
she coughs a little chokes on her own spit
the night nurse didn't hear the radio
was turned on loud she's kind of scared and sorry
and puts a rose on the poor old lady's pillow
and a mortician calls and tells us not to worry
above the sunlit bay the slicing planes
rise fast and one speeds east with her "remains"

14

Back among her belongings her remains
glide north northwest in a shiny SUV
designed to weather snowstorms freezing rains
far from the simmering fields of Sicily
the East Coast cemetery's stony pressed
into a cleft of hills black ice I skid on
leaning to greet the freckled hearty priest
looking not looking at the box she's laid in
at the edge of the polished boards that hold her
    husband
the priest says the words she scorned she didn't believe
(she has to be blessed to belong to holy ground)
and O she would scold us if she were still alive!
no *Tuono di dio* no bolt so fierce and true
as the light of her mind that felt that thought that knew

"ADD FINOCCHIO SEEDS TO YOUR PASTA SAUCE FOR THAT REAL SICILIAN FLAVOR!"

Its humble gray black kernels
nubs of the taste of what *was*
jostling in a jar
on the shelf of the *alimentari,*

                    tell me what Proust knew,
                    and Persephone,
                    how history can
                    shrink to a seed:

the enormous stalking
light, the feathery
evanescent green of let's say
just outside Agrigento

                    packed into a tiny
                    stage set—gesturing tenors,
                    little flares of
                    the tarantella—

at the wrong
end of the opera glass . . .
But O but drop just three
seeds into the pot

               where beef blood broods
               and olive gold, and red and
                   green
               of the garden,
               and out bloom all the giants:

the histrionic cousins
stamping in the kitchen,
the mothers
railing or weeping,

               and the broken ones—
               Cristoforo deported, dying
               alone in Rome,
               mad Liborio who put his fist

through the window
("*Finocchio!*"
"He thought he was a girl!"),
and Eddie, back from the Great War,

who saw his mother
wrapped in black that said
"Your papa's dead"—
and "groaned and fell to the
    floor in a faint"—

and behind them the long steep street,
Strada del Purgatorio
in Sambuca di Sicilia,
just another outpost

                        of the past inside
                        the seed inside
                        the sauce, the wine,
                        the bread, beside

the tall ruins
of the Temple of Concord,
the Arab traders, the faint
mysterious uncles.

SHE WAS

so virginal through all
the graying years of mama
and papa in the cluttered

immigrant apartments, dense
with textures of that other, unlived
European life, its embroidered

cloths, its porcelains and silvers,
to be uselessly, meticulously
tended—mended, polished—

in the smoky evenings home
from work—
and then was suddenly already

sixty-four when the colostomy
turned her inside
out, as if the body

had to be warned that sooner
rather than later
this flesh would be

beside itself
with grief, with bearing
the visible weight

of its own sad
wastings—stench
of perpetual

daughterhood, clench
of the love she
gave to the saints

of love instead of
herself, the love
sucked up into ash-

trays full of
dead Pall Malls—
and at the comatose

end perhaps was
just for a second
p'tite Louise again

in the organdy communion
dress or at the crest
of the stony

hill just outside
Nice, where Tante Rosette
told her to choose

her favorite *lapin*
and gleeful amid
sunny simmering

thyme she didn't
understand quite yet
that *tante* and mama

meant to fix that special
delicious gift
for supper. . . .

    —in memory L.O.M., d. 1976

"NO THANK YOU, I DON'T CARE FOR ARTICHOKES,"

decreed my mother-in-law as my husband
passed the platter of inward-turning
soft-skulled Martian baby
heads around the table,

and they were O so shyly slyly
jostling each other with their boiled-
green sardonic gossip
(what was the news they told?)

when he sharply answered, "Mother,
have you *ever*
eaten an artichoke?"
                    "No,"

she said, majestic, "but I just know
I don't *care* for them, don't
care for them at all"—
for truly, if they weren't Martian,

they were at the least Italian,
from that land of "smelly cheese"
she wouldn't eat, that land of oily
curves and stalks, unnerving pots

of churning *who knows what*,
and she, nice, Jewish, from the Bronx,
had fattened on her Russian-
Jewish mother's *kugel*, kosher

chicken, good rye bread. . . .
Bearded, rosy, magisterial
at forty-five, he laughed,
kept plucking, kept on

licking those narcissistic
leaves, each with its razor point
defending the plump, the tender
secret at the center, each

a greave or plate of edible
armor, so she smiled too,
in the flash of dispute,
knowing he'd give her ice cream later,

all she wanted, as the rich
meal drew to an end
with sweets dished out in the lamplit
circle, to parents, children, grandma—

the chocolate mint she craved,
and rocky road he bought especially
for her, whose knees were just
beginning to crumble from arthritis,

whose heart would pump more creakily
each year, whose baby
fat would sag and sorrow
as her voice weakened, breathing

failed until she too
was gathered into the same
blank center
where her son

at sixty bearded still, still
laughing, magisterial
(though pallid now)
had just a year before

inexplicably settled.

CHOCOLATE

In the end, in the long-term
wing of the assisted living
home, in the small white chamber

looking out on the patio's locked-in
blooms or in the big plain
"day room" with its blaring

TV and hopeful posters,
they fed my mother
ground-up piles of pallid

stuff in bowls clamped onto
a plastic tray and at first
she smiled, *delicious, delicious,*

as she sucked the oozing
juices, the last pap,
smiling surrounded by fellow

diners drooping and mumbling
in their places until
after a while she tightened

her lips against the food and
instead began unknotting,
unknotting the flowered

gown, unclothing her wasting
nakedness still white and smooth
and then at the very end,

when dreamy and slim
as a teen she welcomed
old friends and relatives who flickered

on the walls, the curtains
of the tiny room, nodding,
hello, sit down, to the shiny

nothing, she'd eat nothing
but chocolate, only chocolate,
so every day I brought an oblong

Lindt or Hershey
and square by square
she took in mouthfuls,

smiling and nodding, square
by square, *delicious, dear,*
until she finally

swallowed the whole dense bar.

HELL IS

where you still are
who you are,
what you were,

where you can never
become just
your suffering, the mere pure

flame that cleanses,
never the oblivion
said to smooth some pain

as if the wound should spurt
its own narcotic—
no, you're you,

and what has been
still is:
               a punishment

for nothing you can
understand yet nonetheless
a punishment, especially

that one keen instant
every year (or is it
every day?) when

the door of the iron
prison ratchets back
and you look in

(or is it out?)
and see your children
as they were

(or as they are?)
tiny and hopeful in their
flowered snowsuits

side by side
as if for a casual
snap a minute

just a single one
before the hail of arrows
rises, hisses, flashes

into the flowers, the flesh.

REMNANT

Remember the leftover
square of carpet you
unfolded in my office thirteen
years ago, two years before

the deadly surgery? Remember
how you said it would make the clinical
white tiles "homier"?
Well, yesterday I just

glanced over at it
as I sat writing at the shiny
steel Humanities
Center desk, & I noticed

for the first time that its tawny
skin had thickened—nearly
fogged—with dirt:
"So have it cleaned," you said

in a not dead voice that's still
inside me somewhere,
& O then thirty years of
home unfolded

in me too, home of simmering
lamplight buried & forgotten,
& I stared hard with smarting
eyes at the tattering

remnant that's still
some sort of gold (though graying)
at the center but now
entirely ashen

at the edges.

"IT'LL BE REABSORBED,"

she said when she
told me about the one

that died at eight weeks while
its twin still flourished.

(As if she were a sponge?)
And I remember that I saw it

once for a pulsing minute
on the TV screen—

a pale grub, thumbnail-small,
coiled around a fleeting

heartbeat, hung an inch or so
in the flailing shadows

from another, same size
grub, both sounding steady

staccato signals
like mini spaceships.

"They say," she said,
"this is the way it is

in nature: the weak lose
so the strong can live."

Accept it,
I told myself.

Disengage.
Think of the comfort—

the plushy bloody walls
those not-yet lips would kiss,

and the relief of melting,
flake by flake, cell by cell,

into a dim
maternal churning,

along with all the other losers.

ON THE BEACH

This is the beach where the speckled seals each spring
lie birthing and nursing, mounds of fishy milk
flung into dugouts in the sand, all suckling
pups—a row of mamas tired and stuck,
an outer ring of baby blobs, unsure
what next except the slithery teat, the feed
and the shiny briny *other* stuff not far
away—the cold they're going to have to ride.
  I'll try to stay as still as that: a different
  kind of mom but maybe one who'll learn
  to seem like them, so bland and innocent.
  The glittering water-spray leaps high, fans thin.
  What if the trance of calving time is gone?
  Can I picnic on the shifting sands alone?

II | A Little Night Music

A LITTLE NIGHT MUSIC

1   NIGHT ARRIVAL IN THE TROPICS

where a thick black looms
in loops and tangles

where the dark
thrusts of palm

pierce deeper dark
of swamp and sky

where air
is an oil and a

humming whispering clicking
springs from mud from wind

from sliding
water and stands around

big and loose-
limbed in the casual

shadows leaning
now then

closer to touch
to stroke

the wildest
skin the

rainiest places

who think they're birds
(though they live,

says the maid,
à terre, pas dans les arbres)

squatting among the tall
grass juices

and shrilling their fierce
intermittent claims—

c'est moi, oui, oui, ici,
moi, oui, ici—then

quickly, tinily
harkening each

to each—*toi? oui?*—
among the intricate knots

of insect syntax
shrilling, trilling,

declaiming
oui, moi, ici—et toi?—

so stubborn that even
a stranger on this island

knows: if small curled
fallen leaves could

(heaven forbid)
cry out in the night,

they wouldn't cry like this

3   NIGHT COW

munching the roadside
humped and horny,

mournful and O so *désolée*—
under a buttery grinning

moon, without
a moo of her own, she

wants and wants in
a belly of silence,

wants, white
ghost of a past that had,

said the guide, few "coos,"
a future of silvery

grasslands somewhere
else, instead must wait

and wade here, night after
night, through prickles

and puddles of darkness, under
a dizzy

umbrella of stars,
devouring patches of weedy

black until her skinny
milk comes

pouring out for
no one at least for

nothing she can name.

4   *NIGHT PUNCH, NIGHT*

syrup of crimson, sweet
unassuageable *rouge*

in the long still
throats of the spinning

dark under
cloud froth—

bloom of black
sugar ripened to

petals of rum to
sniff to

swallow and breathe—
and the sleepers plummet

toward what is
lost and soft,

through snorting through
wallow through deepest

forget—as if there weren't
right now, clear on the other

side of things
the same old salt-

white light
bleaching the same old naked

sea-bones shrunk
and stranded

on dry white heights.

MATHEMATICIANS ASLEEP ON THE BEACH
IN GUADALOUPE

Lemmas relinquish their links, theorems
dissolve as the geometers, the algebraists

snuggle into the sand, their rosy
shoulders slick with tropical

oils glowing scarlet, small tight
mounds of buttocks

softening, and long
legs frilled with coarse dark

hairs relaxing
into diagonals.

Firm as the truths on which
they rest, behold

the many-particled strand
unknotting itself as well,

blithe mimic,
sliding with infinite carelessness

into the boil and churn of the sea,
while the mathematicians,

cosy as babies,
let it go, give it up,

forgetting, thoughtless,
even the strong force

that shaped their last conjectures.

ROLLERBLADERS IN PARIS

Unearthly lightness air and speed
of the passionate *rollers* beside the Seine,

always on the *qui vive* along the quais,
as if fleeing into a streak of paint

to be slashed across crude blanks of the material
world by some postmodern Caillebotte,

or better still as if right here, right now
might come the magic liftoff

moment when a dozen *jeunes*
jetting past slow-stepping grandmother

Seine in her shawl of mud
might rise—strange spacecraft!—

into the unimaginable *avenir*
that's coming soon like a full eclipse

above the downward stones of Notre Dame.
But what of the onetime "soaring arches,"

the aching theological erections?
Well, what *of* them?

There's no god but speed hum the tiny
efficient wheels, the hovering blades,

no god but the body that flashes away
and away from its own dead weight,

the glisten of flesh
that rockets past itself

in the mad glad
minute surpassing gravity.

"SEVENTEEN" IN THE MARAIS

Sticky masses of
horn drum string
slamming into the seventeenth-
century stone

cellar walls
as if it were, say,
1950 and turtlenecks
still serious and black

still existential
and the drunken stoned
American drummer
keeping perfect

imperfect
time that's the
four four
four four
and an extra beat

conceived by the cute
Greek cellist
(in the number
he calls "Seventeen")

regales us desultory
listeners nursing old
whiskey with jokes
and apologies

when suddenly
the virtuoso
Potts the leader
tearing into his

tenth white wine
breaks out
into a riff of sweat
playing virtually

two horns at once

the alto sax around
his neck and the soprano
in his hand
while the drummer bares

his teeth and bangs
and the tall electric
guitarist with his
face of Leonardo

angel is dancing
in place as he
pumps his electric
pedals and the contrabassist

tiny and squarely
Irish is dancing too above
his heavy difficult strings
while the piper's pipings blare

ahead of them all

as banging and blaring
they dance straight
toward us and our forgotten
whiskey as if they'd jumped

all dancing
with drums and trumpets
out of the *ancien*
murs of the deep

marais the damp
abiding cellar
under the cellar
where rose-faced and sweaty

with gleaming horns
and stranger instruments
clattering pounding pulsing
the dead

might still rise up.

APRIL IN

California the executive
at her sunstruck computer April

in Paris the cool concierge
at the green door and in Florence

a maiden among the heavy
frames the dark oils and April

the sly one in New York just
turning the corner not too

conspicuous no a little
sinister in trenchcoat and silver-

blue and April O April hot
and panting a bitch sprawled

out in the *zocalo* of Mazatlan
and stark shark naked

on the yellow beaches of Kauai
yet still so queenly in Kirkenes

where just now the pillow of sleep
stirs cracks splits

into the bodies of a dozen
ghostly crocuses

ST. PETERSBURG MOSQUITOES ARE REALLY

tiny drifting souls of the tsars, diminutive
debris of the revolution, hanging out

around the bureaucratic palaces, flicking
like gray-haired shooting stars among

the gun-dark cabinets, the guards
posing as ordinary women, the cafés

drowning in sour cream and soured
spirits: this one over here,

this one is Peter the Great,
now Peter the Infernally Small,

boring into the nerve at a tourist's wrist
with miniature tools—and *this* one,

this nearly invisible one is
onetime puffed-up Catherine,

laying down the law
with the sting of her snout, her knout,

massing flotillas of courtiers
amidst the shimmer that once was hers,

and flickering, panicky,
along the scummy banks of the Neva

as it coils through white
night after night,

or hovering, vengeful shadow,
desperate to flesh out

gilt with blood,
above the black hulk

of the treacherous *Aurora*.

PETERHOF

Framed up in gold, tsarinas rule the walls,
opaque Cyrillic characters adrift
like swans still preening, queenly though bereft
among the weedy fountains, ponds, and falls
where their palace's leftover grandeur
tumbles down the hill as if to fling
the glittering *salons*, the whole shebang
(the flowering china, china flowers, rare
old lacquers, satins, even the bloody ground)
into the flat blank Gulf of Finland:
there hydrofoils rear up on delicate stalks
and circling gulls shriek above the docks
   and new girls leap like trout in icy brine,
   stripped of almost everything but time.

SALOME

The tiny encampment in the desert.
Sheepskin, goatskin, and other goods
people of consequence might wear

to please the gods. The gods.
The heavy sky of the old god,
thrashing with commands.

The parents. Herodias
in glittering stones. Herod
twitching in his golden chair.

The worrying Jews, the smirking
Romans, the swaying
voluptuous eunuchs.

The naked teenage princess
writhing in the prophet's blood.
The head of the prophet, spurting

displeasure. The moon
rising and fattening, the moon
falling and turning, thinning.

The old god, sulking
in his celestial cave, seriously
shifting clouds and constellations,

planning more, still more.

AT GIVERNY, ON CANVAS,

day and night, the little
bridge with its wooden
purposes, its

cultured vain
geometry,
struggles to frame

the great loose
flood and lapse
of light, the stream

now pink
now dark
where tiny creamy

somethings
open and quickly
flare their crimson tips

IN MY JAZZ

poem at Yoshi's he
might be late sixties, seventy, because now the real
geniuses are mostly geezers (as Coltrane

would be if he hadn't marched
to sainthood) and so this one—burnished
skin, shock of silver

hair and elderly
shoulders suited sober
smoking-jacket black—

this one begins to hop
and pop and heavy breathe into
his shiny aging beatnik

sax under the shiny
Xmas lights and now
he's dancer and prancer airily

hauling the music into its only
accurate place and now he's
heaving all that thinning

calcium up and down,
the skeleton
climbing out of the tune,

the who knows what
("on the human journey")
bobbing and jumping just

in front of the velvet
curtain, the dark
lenses flashing black

before our very eyes.

—*Charles Lloyd at Yoshi's, January 4, 2002*

III | Four Masks

FOUR MASKS

1

First the fish that cling to your slithery
skin (who knows how?), your shapely

skull—its "forehead," its "cheekbones,"
its fated lines and planes—

plastered with your own sweet shining
outside, then with minnows, sea trout, glittering

silver of salmon spawn,
to guide you through the black and churn

of the heavy waters, up and up
to the knife of light at the top.

2

Then bear snout, the rubbery freight
of nostrils and jowls, a fat

pack that drags your whole hot pulsing
head straight down like a magnet tracking

elemental traces—
and prickles of fur stand on your surfaces,

and you prowl, cloaked in meat,
through sore, through wanting, through inescapable
    weight,

into a thicket where every drop of blackberry sweetness
only opens another trail into emptiness.

3

Oh then bird-shape, sleek, aerobic,
glued to your right eye as if it were a lens to trick

you into feathers, turn you into the showy
winged thing you're looking through—a snowy

egret, dove, gull, parrot. . . . *Now*
you vow to "dart" and "soar" and "throw"

your all across the sky, as if—as if
the very thought of lift

could hurl you into a heaven
beyond the stone, the given.

4

At last a butterfly?
Twin loops that say "infinity"?

How beautiful to look at you've become,
eyes shaped by leaves of flame,

brow guarded by quivering symbols
of what just maybe might escape the shambles

where fish- bear- bird-flesh rot and stink!
In thinnest air you rise! Or won't you for a minute sink

to envy the lucky caterpillars far below
who still have the whole unfolding to look forward to?

EMPIRE STATE

where dull as an old rug a winter
sunset settles over
the late city,

its million microscopic
fires fluttering
out and far—and far

down there
a blare and blur
of scuttling

things inaudible
as high and higher
you go in the windy

dark and lifted
to an icy
platform, look!

the blur and scuttling
isn't even motion
anymore or line

but just a barely
visible distance
into down

and down though once,
or is it somewhere,
there's a long

wide prairie,
endless grasses
seething—

and at the center
a broad square clapboard
house, higher

than you could even see.

SUNDAY MORNING AND

like a two-toed sloth you
dangle in a tidy
jar of sleep, sleep

accretes around you—
expensive honey,
thick and sticky-sweet—

so over and over again
you dip, you lick,
though just outside

the rain is busy
weaving a shawl of dark
canals around the house,

and the garden is turning
into little Venice, little
Amsterdam, except

without traditions,
since after all the gods
packed up their vast majestic

bags some centuries ago,
and now not a single black umbrella
sets off down the hill to church. . . .

Why bother to stand
upright on a day like this?

Why not just bury your
snout in utter honey?

Old leaves are shredding
in the canals, and the streets
are full of strange debris.

SKUNK

1

A sudden stink so vast it seems some demon's
raised a spirit wall around the house.
And you say, *It's* in *the house!*

Its cuddle of color scuttling
in the basement? Its ill will
set against our snores?

Now the moving moon peers down
through a low barred window
to where a pelt of riddle

looms between the box the toaster came in
and the broken Exercycle.

2

Nothing paces the meadow, nothing
tramples the brush, scurries
under the deck—

                    only
the stench of *could it be*—?
acrid and everlasting

films the air,
untouchable as moonlight.

3

The river leans against its bank,
the ocean obsessively reiterates itself,

the trees erect their trunks, unfold
their ebony branches

and a furry yearning
creeps out of the windbreak,

the skunk is foraging,
has foraged, will—

4

Jawbone and clavicle
strewn
beside the hot tub,

black boat of the sun
where the skunk is riding,
a streak of white light

down the center. . . .

MATRIARCH

Archaic dog jaw pig snout
emerging resolute

from decades of silence
from veils of dutiful

beauty and the eyes
set deep in their rings

the neck erect as if
proud as if grand

with the ache of
time worn through

the shoulders stooped
for the cape of

stiffness meant to settle
across them

the breasts still full still
tense with their history

of languor of tender or tooth-
grinding hunger the belly

a slack and careless white
above scars above

patchy baldness mapping
the hill of love

and under the hill
a rage to feed and be

fed and behind the eyes
in their rings of wrinkles

tears of the tumbling litter
and under the snout

a hint of whiskers
and in the throat

the start of a howl

THE TALL PALE

grasses
hiss in the wind,
they bow and quiver as if in

fear or joy when
cold fingers of light
comb through them

telling each:
here in this mass of selves
you are single, you are

singular—
          the grasses sway
and jostle, together,

apart, together,
apart:
          if they were tall pale

threads of tin or silver rather than
seed, husk, fiber,
they'd clash and tinkle

like gamelan gongs
as the insubstantial
pranced among them,

step after spooky
step on its path
to nowhere—

and under its emptiness
new somethings,
undefinable

nubs that might be
sprouts of
stem or moss keep

rising, dragging
savory bodies
upward, anyway!

Riding the broad back of
a rain-soaked log
fixed deep

in the green at
the edge of the cliff,
who wouldn't

wonder at such wild
behavior?—
the whole meadow,

its dying grasses clashing
and preening
above their young,

casting a net of freshness
toward the sea—
the way, say,

toward the end
of the wedding lunch
a gray-haired great aunt

might be caught
hip-hopping
in her satin frock

with a not quite teenage
nephew, his feet
in shiny new shoes

beating the ballroom floor,
shadows gathering
outside the tall pale

ballroom windows

MORNING AGAIN

and the rain is walking around
out there,

at first we hear only a slow few distant
footsteps, the sad

track of a limping
spirit circling

the house, searching, testing
the walls, the windows:

then as we turn
in the bed, half blind

with sleep and a little
trouble, as we wake

to the thin gray
morning slicing

into the blue stripes
of the curtains, a sudden

tumble of urgent tiny
knocks begins,

as if to say,
we're here and we aren't you,

we're here,
and we're no one you know,

and though you huddle
under the motherly

puff of the coverlet, yes,
for no discernable reason

on this particular morning
we are driven

toward you in multitudes.

CHAIRLIFT

What does it allegorize, such unseemly
haste at the beginning
and the end—

the swift attendants gripping, heaving
each of us
into a steady place,

and then the long slow silent
journey over
and up the mountain, swaying

in sunshine or buffeted
by churning
winds, the sea beyond, with its tiny

sails and lonesome
cloudscapes, and all along,
under the bob of the shadow

that hangs below every chair,
a real live human
world of vines and gardens

boiling and blooming and getting
sparser as the humming
cables clamber

higher, steeper, until
soon there are only empty
meadows, knots of forest, channels

of frigid
granite or ice,
though just before someone suddenly

drags you off
at the summit,
just before the circling seats

descend for another
round, you notice
lying in the last deep

weedy cutbank,
all by itself,
one mateless leather clog. . . .

DADDY LONG LEGS, DAWDLING,

delicate in the tub, with fine
long threads of motion only just so
gently lifting & drifting across

the ivory damp—
                    O how can I
spill a splash of killing

water over this languorous
insect self that might be
you (as once I thought

for months after we buried you
that every speck & splotch
of palpitating

life was you in whatever
mote you could
find to stick your spirit to),

and now though this dawdling
daddy isn't you, the father
of my son & daughters,

still, how like in life
& liveliness & long fine
legs he is, reminding me

how once on long
fine legs, with certain
steps you walked, reminding

me even in the way
he rises, insouciant, along
the slippery walls

of the tub of the way
you walked, the way
each morning from your bed

you rose insouciant,
you rose,
you walked.

LESSON

Two days past Hallowe'en, a day after
the Day of All Souls, not raining yet
in dusty California.

                 No, my daughter
said, *no, don't call him the father, no, just
call him the donor.*

                 She stood in her burgeoning
garden, my baby grandson on her hip,
the leaf, the blossom, and the bole still urgent

round her, snail tracks on the stones, and lots
of other shining things to make the baby
laugh and clap.

                 What's the difference, I wondered,
brooding on "the mystery
of paternity." She frowned.

                 A father
fathers, *mom*, she said. *A donor just, well,
donates stuff. We call him Biopop.*

Lurid cardboard pumpkins, bright black cats
and witchy hats plastered the picture window.
The baby beamed and pointed.

                              Does anything loom
at the edge of the flickering green
he sees?

            No Father fathering—maybe
only a Donor just donating stuff,
some kind of Biopop . . . ?

                        Overhead
a few new sodden clouds sailed high and higher,
bellies thick with unrained rain.

FEBRUARY AND THE OAK MOTHS

bloom among the big dark
trunks that guard the winter
garden: at night

when the house is lit and moist
with its own
ideas of food and sex

they enter, they insert their little
plaintive flappings
between the white hot

bulbs of the lamps
and the shades, as if
they were old souls, the slightly

aging parchment-yellow
souls of our own
dead, slightly soiled, slightly

worn with all those
memories that drew them
out of the trees, out of the larval

stupor where they hung
forgetful until
February urged them

back to the light, the
heat, the wet—
grandma Bob Elliot Virginia Richard

impossible
to name them
all in their single annual

minute winging
through the doorway
until they die again,

again become crisp
shells of themselves—
and we can't help

stepping on them,
can't help that as we
pass above them, squeamish, they

crackle like fallen leaves.

WHAT EXTENDS

a bony finger just now just
outside the glass-paned door
from deck to kitchen?

As if it were a breezy
shake of the hand, a chill
hello from a not

unfriendly passer-
by in the night,
the skinny thing knock-

knocks, it wants to be
friends with the one
who huddles alone

in the house, the one
by the oven who
sees just now

that this sudden guest is just
a bamboo wind chime
from holiday

Hawaii telling its usual
tale of the long-ago
tangles of jungle, the vivid

daze of yearning upward, of
scorch and wet and the tickle
of leaves—

and the chopping down and
the change into a skinless
thing that clatters its polish

with every gust, wanting
to show how
bone can speak of

pleasure still, how a dangle
of bones can say,
In my death

I greet you on this wild
night, in my death I prove
dead stems can make

a music of their own.

IV | A Year and a Day

A YEAR AND A DAY

JANUARY MEADOW,

whistles and simmers in the low, south-sliding
California sun, creak of crows
in hedgerows, bristle of grasses still abiding
winter pallor, silence of cypresses
upholding sheaves of needles—*here they are!*—
like gifts of darkness to a sky whose light's
so fierce and clear it arches toward forever
in the tiny shine of noontime minutes.
The tree guy's dragged and dumped the tree that toppled
last week (when the power failed). Let's gather
sunshine now, lounge in the hot tub, tipple
a little, watch the twelve o'clock news together—
(peace marchers shouting in the city
under a sky like this, so blue, so pretty. . . .)

FEBRUARY GRASS,

and each blade burns green as if in Richard Dadd's
meticulous mad miniatures, each pebble
flanks the light that's everywhere and threads
its glistening through stone and stick and stubble.
And you: do you love this shining still, or curse
the radiant flash and jolt you can't have back
now that you're just an empty suit, or worse,
stuck in a box that's stuck in a cake of muck?
Some say the raging dead howl and haunt
because they hate us so—the heat, the weight
that let us move the way they won't and can't.
Some say they wing like moths into our light.
    And some might say you nibble these skinny roots
    as shining grasses hug my winter boots.

MARCH MOON,

coats the meadow with a film of silver-
gray—old-lady hair on Mother Earth:
a faery mom from Walter de la Mare
or witchy snag-toothed rock-browed Lilith?
Nights like these, when even in New York
the sky was lit like a phantom sidewalk, these
were the times my real-life mom would scream and
    shriek
in nightmares whose wild echoes made me freeze
in my little-girl bed in my silvery little-girl room.
What was scaring her, what did she know just then?
I clung to my pillow, prayed I wouldn't dream—
and the high moon paled and got faraway and thin
    above the empty streets four stories down
    where every streetlight whitened like a moon.

APRIL HEART-

beat in the greening field, drops of vibes
jumping as if Bobby Hutcherson himself
rained rhythm on the stones, great silver globes
of sound, each trickle fattening each leaf,
and those camellias in the garden bloom
like showy drumming, crimson-pink, enormous,
and the lush life tippling in the stream
repeats itself again, again—ground bass.
O wild and whistling western wind, be thou
a saxophone to wake the meadow up,
and you, O hissing cypresses, be you
big brushy strokes of kindness root to tip!
    Bobby's breathing hard, the drumming's fast.
    Some tulip's leaping somewhere. Let this last!

MAY SEED,

seed of hay, úp stárt starting
up from scratch-the-bark, scratch-in-the-grass,
scratch-the-tight-wád-of-pulp just tilting
slightly skyward like a microfleece
unfolding micro meadow, micro *maybe
this will last*—fellow upstart, how
soon will your meadow grow from plushy baby
stuff to big tough green to dry to fallow
under a ceiling of big tough stars that wheel,
old robots—always churning always there—
behind the stupid blue you think is real,
the blue you trust, the sun you trust, the air?
    Carpe something while you can, young thing,
    before the sky gets back to bullying!

JUNE—NOON

of buttery melt in the welter of leaves, the sticky
sidle or clamber toward "heaven" (or any yellow
whatever) and now the grown-up eggs in plucky
numbers tensing in the prickle and hollow
of anybody's nest, are almost ready
to float a whole new gendering of trebles
over the mole scars, under the high and steady
scope of crows, skyscape of peering eagles. . . .
Dear Emily, you said it so much better:
you watched the eggs fly off in music, praising
the truthful hills as you cleared the kitchen clutter,
measuring language, weighing and sifting the phrasing.
   Old friend, the noon of June is out of tune
   unless you stir it with your silver spoon.

JULY, AND A WHOLE

month past the solstice with its rites and mights,
its *anything you can do I can do just as well*
or nearly so) and the weeds writhe up and the nights
flash black a little longer, only a little.
Who cares? We've stoked the coals for the barbecue,
brewed the beer for the same Last Chance Café
we open every year—and you, and *you:*
go get inseminated now! today!
The builders build, the knockers down knock down,
the nations rage together in the grass,
and the pine cones, ancient, Fibonaccian,
unfold their clever codes next to the house.
   If we leave them alone, they'll prosper—delve and
         thrive—
   and turn into somebody else's sacred grove.

AUGUST IN THE OLD, GOLD

hotel, and everybody packing up
(or un-) or hanging towels on the railings,
and the noisy buzz of insects doesn't stop,
and the whoosh of fans stirs cobwebs on the ceilings.
Down in the kitchen the sweaty pastry chef
is getting sick of pie crusts, sick of *sticky!*
It's only a summer job: she wants to stiff
the management, go back to school, get lucky.
And the geezers on the beach play cards all day,
slapping down aces under the honey sun
like dopes, thinks the pastry chef, as she rolls the dough
and slides another something into the oven.
   Shouts of kids in the lake in the sunset haze.
   Goodbyes on the porch. Clack clack of hovering
      crows.

SEPTEMBER LIGHT

that glazes you in the ripeness of what was,
and you so gold and rose now in the blue
cube of the pool, your blooming daughters in place
around you like mild naiads, drifting and slow—
you, breathing the late heat, side-
stroking in and out of the quiver-tremble
that's now clear depth and now a slice of shade
(and here you're lazy, here a minute nimble)—
this light of September thickens, weighs you down:
even as you glide in glistering blue,
all insubstantial soul and airy skin,
the sun you love's a Midas gilding you,
    then turning you solid gold, its alchemy
    killing you (coolly) into history.

OCTOBER MIST

of cobwebs drifting in the yard, fence
to mailbox, bush to gate to who knows where
in see-through loops as if the whole damn place
had been wrapped and sealed by a master packager.
And even the insect nations are quieter now
(except for a few last loutish clots of bees),
waiting behind the scrolls and veils for how
and how soon the chill will quicken, juices freeze.
Slowing down inside the walls of hush,
even the daisies look a little sick:
their heads are heavy, only the wind is "fresh."
They seem to want to complain, to hiss *Hey, don't talk*
about design, even if you think all this
is part of some infinite mystery plan for bliss.

NOVEMBER TREE FERN,

out of time and place, with your grace
of not belonging (and your pineapple bottom,
wings unfurling into intricate space)
you must have come from somewhere slow and solemn.
Archaic headdress fixed on nothing, how
can you erect your feathers on our deck?
Here comes grandma—pumpkins, mistletoe,
cartoon balloons of breath, her icy *shtick*—
and you don't care, don't bloom, you *never* bloom,
(why risk a flower now? why invest?)
you just keep on unfurling, always the same,
and leave that cyclical nonsense to the rest.
    All Souls, All Saints pass over in a wind.
    Indifferently, you stand your different ground.

DECEMBER SEA,

ice-light on its greén gráy skin,
wrinkles of glitter looking nearly Arctic
beyond the pound and flail that's coming in
above a hiss of silence drawing back—
and out on the bluff, in the vast wind, the whole
ensemble flashes meaning, as if an alien
scientist had planned a mystic signal
he then forgot, but *it* went on and on. . . .
Though from the house the signal's just some glints
outside the window of the steamy kitchen
where the baby rules us like a cranky prince
who squeaks and squalls and suckles: (except when
   we kiss him, jog him, pass him back and forth
   he gazes vaguely up, and out, and north).

FEBRUARY 11, 2003

So moist and warm after a dozen years
(though why should the season have gotten any colder?)
but the cypress we planted to screen our house from
    neighbors
split during last week's storm—as in *Jane Eyre!*—
its white theatrical wound a jagged plane
for not-a-word to crawl on, not a life,
and where the branches stood not a thing has grown
the way it did when I was still your wife.
"Do you stress the *volta?*" someone asked at a reading,
"do your sonnets turn and change after the octave?"
Stuck in the sestet, stuck in the downward sliding,
what answer, darling, could I think or give?
    Uncouplings shatter the couplet, but in the end,
    in the empty, there isn't room to turn around.

    —*In memory of E.L.G., d.* 2/11/91

THE NEW TREE

knows the pain of inching into life:
its new buds seem to swell like nubs of blood
on the arms of the Y of sticks that stand so light
and all alone in a flattened-out black plot.
Not a speck of green in the three-foot-wide surround
of soil James the gardener hacked and raked—
it's too soon, even here, for weedy ground;
just time for these twigs of plum to trickle red
into little spots of blossom—then the pink
innocuous petals ruffling in the yard,
pastel baby banners of a spring
of purple leaves that haven't happened yet,
    though somewhere in, or under, the flayed thin
    skin of the new tree they wait and plan.

ACKNOWLEDGMENTS

"What extends," "February and the oak moths," "Belongings," "St. Petersburg mosquitoes are really," "Peterhof," "Afternoon walk: the sea ranch," and "February 11, 2003" all first appeared in *Poetry*. "Chocolate" and "Remnant" first appeared in *TriQuarterly*. "A Little Night Music" first appeared in the *Virginia Quarterly Review*. "Four Masks," "Chairlift," and "The tall pale" first appeared in the *Ontario Review*. "'Add finocchio seeds to your pasta sauce for that real sicilian flavor'" and "'No thank you, I don't care for artichokes'" first appeared in *The Milk of Almonds: Italian American Women Writers on Food and Culture*, ed. Louise DeSalvo and Edvige Giunta (New York: Feminist Press, 2002), and then in Sandra M. Gilbert, *The Italian Collection* (Mill Valley: Depot Books, 2003). "Skunk" first appeared in *Field*. "January meadow," first appeared in *100 Poets Against the War*, ed. Todd Swift (Cambridge, U.K.: Salt Publishing, 2003). "Daddy long legs, dawdling" first appeared in *The Washington Square Review*.

Warmest thanks to my poetry group—Chana Bloch, Jeanne Foster, Diana O'Hehir, Peter Dale Scott, Phyllis Stowell, Mark Turpin, and (especially) Alan Williamson, along with (when we're lucky enough to have her with us) Shirley Kaufman—and thanks, too, to Mary Turnbull of Depot Books, as well as to my faithful constant reader, David Gale.